The Official Guide to Home Inspections

The Official Guide to Home Inspections

Knowing and Playing by the Rules

Chris Perry

America's Home Inspection Referee

Dedication

I dedicate this book to my mom and dad,
Johnny and Jewerl Perry.

And a special thanks to Tommy Sproles and all the others who have helped me along the way.

You know who you are.

TGBTG = "To God Be the Glory"

Chris Perry

Table of Contents

List of Abbreviations

AFCI	arc-fault circuit interrupter
ASHI	American Society of Home Inspectors
CRI	Certified Real Estate Inspector
EPA	Environmental Protection Agency
EBPHI	Examination Board of Professional Home Inspectors
EIFS	exterior insulation and finish systems
FEMA	Federal Emergency Management Agency
GFCI	ground-fault circuit interrupter
HVAC	heating, ventilation, and air conditioning
ICC	International Code Council
InterNACHI	International Association of Certified Home Inspectors
NAHI	National Association of Home Inspectors
NHIE	National Home Inspector Examination
NRPP	National Radon Proficiency Program
WDO	wood-destroying organism

List of Figures

Preface

Yes, I really am a football referee, and being one has helped me become a great home inspector. Whether I walk onto a football field to referee a game or into a home to perform a home inspection, my objective is the same: to serve with integrity, purpose, and gratitude.

As a referee, I observe my surroundings on the football field, focus on the plays, and process the rules of the game. When I spot an infraction, I throw a flag. The same holds true when I inspect a home. As a professional home inspector, I observe the overall condition of the home, focus on the integrity of structures and systems, and process standards of practice in order to identify deficiencies. Both environments require a tremendous attention to detail, a professional set of standards, and the ability to apply the standards consistently and judiciously. During a football game, my eyes are trained to see infractions, and during a home inspection, they are trained to see deficiencies.

The purpose of this book is threefold:

- to educate home buyers and home sellers about the purpose and need for a home inspection,
- to teach home buyers and home sellers how to select the right home inspection partner, and
- to help home buyers and home sellers navigate through and benefit from the home inspection process.

This book is a how-to consumer's guide to home inspections. Anyone who has ever purchased a home or is about to purchase one will benefit from this book. This book not only outlines the essential players and regulators in the home inspection industry it also contains real-world examples, helpful illustrations, and a wealth of practical advice.

Why am I the right person to write this book? The answer is because I bring the right mix of professional experience and practical know-how from working in a variety of home-related industries. As a young man, I worked construction alongside my father. I've been a building inspector for the city of Little Rock, a termite inspector for a national company, and a disaster inspector for FEMA. I even tried my hand as a licensed real estate agent for a short while. After all of these experiences, I discovered that what I really love to do and what I'm really good at is inspecting homes.

The knowledge and experience acquired from fieldwork in other home-related industries enables me to evaluate the condition of a home from a variety of perspectives. Examples in this book show how a $5 solution averted a $5,000 problem, why a new home needs to be inspected just as much as an existing home, and how to view a home from a home inspector's point of view.

Reading this book won't make someone a home inspector any more than reading a football rulebook makes someone a referee. But this book will help home buyers and home sellers make more informed decisions about the real value and actual condition of one of the biggest assets they may ever purchase: A Home.

Section 1: Getting Started

Players in the Game of Buying a Home

Buying a home is a huge investment, and paying a mortgage a huge responsibility. According to United States census data, the average home prices in January 2012 and January 2016 were $265,700 and $365,600, respectively.[1] After controlling for the 2008 crash in the real estate market and the 2009–2011 pricing fallout, there has been a 37 percent increase in the average home price in the United States since 2012. Also according to United States census data, the median household income in 2014 was $53,657: a number that has remained fairly constant since 2012.[2] With home prices on the rise and household income remaining flat, buying the right home at the right price and knowing exactly what you're buying is more important now than ever before.

Buying a home can be a dream come true or a nightmare in the making, and home buyers need to

---

[1] "Median and Average Sales Price of New Homes Sold in United States," United States Census Bureau, accessed April 20, 2016, http://www.census.gov/construction/nrs/pdf/uspricemon.pdf.

[2] "Income and Poverty in the United States: 2014," United States Census Bureau, accessed April 20, 2016, http://www.census.gov/content/dam/Census/library/publications/2015/demo/p60-252.pdf.

pick their partners wisely. A home buyer's selection of the right partners has a huge impact on the process and experience of buying a home. Essentially there are four main players in the game of buying a home:

- The mortgage lender
- The realtor
- The appraiser
- The home inspector

The lender, the realtor, the appraiser, and the home inspector each play a unique and vital role in the transaction of buying a home. Of course, the buyer and the seller are the most important players in the game. But, of all these, the number one player in the game of buying a home is the buyer. The buyer hires the team members and calls all the shots. In football terms, the home buyer is the owner of the football team.

The Mortgage Lender

The mortgage lender is typically one of the first players in the game of buying a home. A home buyer approaches the purchase of a home in much the same way that a potential owner of a football team approaches the purchase of a professional football team: each goes to a lender, expresses an interest in purchasing an asset, and asks to borrow money to make the deal happen. Before looking at homes and even before contracting with a realtor, a home buyer should contact banks or mortgage lenders and get prequalified for a loan.

The lender is the player who valuates the buyer's assets and income to determine how much money to lend the buyer. In other words, the lender determines how much of a home the home buyer can afford. Based on current interest rates, the terms of the selected loan, the home buyer's income, and the home buyer's credit score, the lender will determine the home buyer's affordable monthly payment and then prequalify the home buyer for a specific loan amount based on the affordable monthly payment.

The affordable monthly payment is determined by calculating and comparing two debt-to-income ratios: the front-end ratio and the back-end ratio. The front-end ratio, also called the housing ratio, includes principal, interest, taxes, and homeowner insurance. The back-end ratio includes all the factors in the front-end ratio plus all other debt obligations like car loans and credit card payments. According to bankrate.com, the standard rule for lenders is that the front-end ratio should not exceed 28 percent and the back-end ratio 36 percent.[3] These debt-to-income ratios are ballpark figures. Home buyers should ask prospective lenders what the debt-to-income requirements are for their particular situation.

Here's how to determine how much home a home buyer can afford. Let's say that the lender has determined that the home buyer can afford the monthly payment on a $200,000 mortgage and the lender also requires a 20 percent cash down payment. In this example, a 20 percent down payment is used for illustrative purposes: some down payments may be as low as 5 percent. Be sure to ask your lender about the expected down payment. This means that in this case the home buyer's top price is $250,000. Here's how to back into the top price of a home based on the prequalified mortgage amount.

---

[3] "How Much House Can I Afford?" Bankrate, accessed April 20, 2016, http://www.bankrate.com/calculators/mortgages/new-house-calculator.aspx.

$250,000	Top Price of Home
– ($50,000)	(Minus 20 Percent Down Payment)
= $200,000	= Prequalified Mortgage Amount

The Realtor

Armed with the information about how much of a loan the home buyer can secure, the home buyer then reaches out to a real estate agent. The home buyer informs the real estate agent that they have been prequalified and can afford a home under a certain amount. In this example, the amount is $250,000.

Now the fun begins. The home buyer tells the real estate agent about the size, location, and important features of the home that they wish to purchase, and the agent sets up showings on homes that meet the home buyer's criteria. For example, the real estate agent may set up showings on three-bedroom, two-bath, two-car-garage homes in certain neighborhoods, subdivisions, or sections of town in the $225,000–$250,000 price range because that is what the home buyer can afford to finance.

Choosing and working with the right real estate agent when buying or selling a home is an important decision. A real estate agent is a state-licensed professional who is schooled in local, state, and national real estate laws. Technically, a *realtor®* is a real estate agent who is a member of the National Association of Realtors, but a real estate agent does not need to be a realtor to be a real estate agent. This book will use the terms interchangeably.

A realtor not only knows how to comply with all the applicable real estate laws and how and when to complete all the necessary paperwork, but also has valuable experience in negotiating contracts. Experience and reputation distinguish one realtor from another. Ask around, and ask friends and family if they have had a good experience with a realtor. Ask a realtor for references. Interview more than one realtor before making a decision about who to do business with.

Remember, the home buyer is the owner of the team, and the realtor works for the home buyer. With the assistance of the realtor, the home buyer decides which home to place an offer on and how much to offer. After an offer is made two things happen: (1)

the lender orders an appraisal, and (2) the home buyer orders a home inspection.

The Appraiser

The lender orders and requires an appraisal. The purpose of the appraisal is to protect the lender. The appraisal sets the value of the home and determines how much the lender will loan against the property. The home must appraise for the offer price to qualify for the full loan amount. If the home appraises for less than the offer amount, the lender will not loan the full amount against the property. If the home appraises for less, the home buyer will be asked to pay the shortfall in cash. For example, if a home listing for $250,000 only appraises for $225,000, the lender will only loan $225,000 less 20 percent down payment, or $180,000 ($225,000 - $45,000 = $180,000). If the home buyer still wants to buy this home, the home buyer will have to pay the down payment plus the shortfall ($45,000 + $25,000 = $70,000) at closing.

If there is any question about whether a home will appraise for at least the offer price, it is prudent to have the appraisal done before the home inspection. Knowing that the lender will not loan the full amount may be a deal-breaker.

The Home Inspector

When buying a home, always have the home inspected. Realtors do not hire professional home inspectors: home buyers and home sellers hire home inspectors. While the appraisal determines the value of the home based on the property's features and location, the home inspection report impacts the value by identifying deficiencies, maintenance issues, or safety concerns that may impact the current value of the property.

A home inspector does not look at the cosmetics of a home. A home inspector does not evaluate the type of windows in a home. A home inspector looks at whether the windows open and close properly, and whether they were installed and have been maintained properly. A home inspector does not care about the color of the home, but a home inspector is greatly concerned about the integrity of the foundation and the roof.

In referee terms, a home inspector looks for deficiencies and brings them to the client's attention much like when a referee throws a flag for an infraction in a football game. A home inspector looks for proper installation of appliances and systems, the presence of proper materials, and signs of improper maintenance and subsequent deterioration—a home inspector looks for deficiencies. A home inspector questions the remaining useful life of major systems and components like roofs and heating and cooling systems and may recommend evaluation by a qualified technician. And a home inspector identifies safety and environmental issues that may not be readily apparent to an untrained eye.

Once an offer is made by the home buyer and accepted by the home seller, the home buyer typically has 10–14 days to have the home inspected and submit a repair addendum to the seller. A repair addendum is a list of deficiencies discovered by a home inspector that a home buyer asks a home seller to remedy in consideration for completing the purchase of the home.

Once the home seller has reviewed and responded to the repair addendum, negotiations between the buyer and seller start. This is when a good realtor is invaluable. Will the seller make any repairs and correct deficiencies? Which repairs, if any, will the seller make and to what extent? If the seller is unwilling to make repairs, is the seller willing to adjust the selling price? These are the questions and conversations that the realtor will help the home buyer navigate.

Specialty Inspectors

There are specialty inspectors to be aware of when buying a home. Specialty inspectors focus on issues that are not included in the scope of a routine home inspection. There are specialty inspectors for a wide variety of purposes and issues; here are some examples:

- Asbestos assessment and abatement professionals
- Code compliance building inspections
- Environmental inspectors: lead, radon, air or water quality
- Exterior Insulation and finish systems (EIFS) inspectors
- Mold assessors and mold remediation professionals
- Pest intrusion or wood-destroying organism (WDO) inspectors
- Special structure inspectors: septic systems, pools, and spas
- Structural inspectors

Many professional home inspectors are trained and certified to perform specialty inspections. Some specialty inspectors are state regulated requiring a separate license like asbestos inspectors and mold assessors in the state of Florida or structural pest inspectors for wood-destroying organisms in the state of Washington. A professional home inspector may be able to conduct a specialty inspection if the inspector has obtained additional training or certification.

For example, a professional inspection or evaluation of a pool or spa requires specialized training and credentials, and a structural inspection requires the expertise of a structural engineer. Structural engineers and pool inspectors often bring years of invaluable experience to bear when identifying the early signs of deterioration or failure. If safety issues are suspected or the integrity of systems outside the scope of a routine home inspection are questioned, contact an experienced professional specialty inspector.

The Huddle: Key Questions for Home Buyers & Home Sellers

This section answers three essential questions that every person buying or selling a home should understand about the home inspection process. Understanding the answer to each of these three questions sets the stage for a successful home inspection game plan. When buying a home, a successful home inspection strategy protects the assets of the home buyer, just like a sound offensive football strategy helps a football team win games.

- What is a residential home inspection?
- Why hire a professional home inspector?
- Why have a home inspected?

What Is a Residential Home Inspection?

A residential home inspection is an objective, visual examination of the readily accessible physical structures and installed systems of a home using normal operating controls at the time of the inspection. The key components of this definition are:

- Visual examination

- Readily accessible
- Physical structures and installed systems
- Normal operating controls
- At the time of the inspection

A residential home inspection is a visual examination or inspection; it is not an analytical or technical examination. A home inspection does not analyze air or water quality, test for the presence of environmental hazards, use infrared technology to detect moisture intrusion, or provide an energy audit. And because a home inspection is a visual examination, not technically exhaustive, the inspection may not identify concealed conditions or latent defects.

A home inspection includes a visual examination of these major components:

- Structure
- Exterior
- Roof
- Plumbing
- Electrical
- Heating and air conditioning
- Interior
- Insulation and ventilation
- Fireplaces and fuel-burning appliances

A home inspection does not include examination of specialty systems like alarm, irrigation, or communication (i.e., telephone, cable, or internet) systems. (Detailed descriptions for each major component of the structures and systems evaluated during a routine residential home inspection are provided in the Routine Home Inspection section of this book.)

A home inspector is expected to evaluate the readily accessible structures and systems of a home using normal operating controls. Readily accessible means that the inspector is not expected to move personal property. And normal operating controls means that a home inspector verifies that an installed appliance turns on and works: all the features and functions are not verified. A routine inspection only includes installed systems and appliances. (See the Routine Home Inspection section, Interiors subsection, for further details about which appliances are included and excluded in a routine home inspection.) And lastly, but most importantly, a home inspection is a snapshot of a home's condition at a point in time. A home inspection and the home inspection report that results reflect the condition of the home at the time of the inspection, not the condition of the home a day, a week, or a moment later.

Like a referee in a football game who throws a flag when a player violates the rules, a professional home inspector not only reports a deficiency, a thorough home inspector also identifies the root cause. While identifying the cause may not be the standard of care throughout the industry, a good home inspector identifies why the problem occurred in the first place, even if additional research or investigation is required.

Know the Cause, Because the Cause Matters

While identifying the cause of a deficiency may not be the standard of care throughout the industry, a good home inspector identifies why the problem occurred in the first place even if additional research or investigation is required.

Even though a professional home inspector may acquire knowledge about home building, home maintenance, and home real estate through years of experience, a professional home inspector should not cross certain business boundaries. A professional home inspector should not offer advice or counsel about the market value, operating costs, or suitability of a home. A home inspector should also not advise a home buyer about whether or not to purchase a property. And lastly, a home inspector is not a building inspector: a home inspector does not advise about compliance with building codes and ordinances.

A visual examination involves the use of sight, sound, smell, and touch. The visual examination begins the minute a home inspector drives up to the property. A good home inspector is noting the pitch of the lot and the placement of the property on the lot. Is there a natural slope for rain to run away from the home rather than running toward the home in a rainstorm?

What is the condition of the landscaping? Is the landscaping interfering with the structure or maintenance of the home? Do shrubbery or trees hang over the roof creating a potential hazard? Are there large established trees too close to the foundation, potentially causing structural issues? These are examples of some of the initial visual notes that a professional home inspector is trained to observe.

As a professional home inspector enters a property, sight, sound, smell, and touch continue to play an important role. Does the home smell musty due to mold or moisture? Does the crawlspace or attic smell of prior or current wildlife or pest intrusion, or are there sounds of a current intrusion?

Baseboard Mystery

Upon entering the living room of a home, I notice some discoloration on the baseboard. Hmmm, I wonder... So I use my screwdriver to gently probe the area. My investigation leads me to suspect termite infestation. I confirm this by noticing mud tubes and termite droppings.

It is not unusual for home buyers and home sellers to view a home radically differently from how a professional home inspector views a home. When the trained eye of a home inspector sees a slight discoloration on a kitchen ceiling or excessive mold in a bathroom, the inspector investigates potential ventilation problems, whereas the home buyer might think, *Gee... the ceiling could use a new coat of paint.* It is incumbent upon the home inspector to notice everything and to determine the root cause of suspicious findings.

Why Hire a Professional Home Inspector?

A residential home inspection should be conducted by a professional home inspector. A professional home inspector has the required training, credentials, and proper perspective to conduct a thorough, objective examination and inspection of a home. A professional home inspector is trained to look for deficiencies due to improper construction, failing systems, improper materials, or inadequate maintenance.

Sometimes it is tempting to consider not hiring a professional home inspector. Thoughts like the following are tempting but potentially very costly. Don't let any of these thoughts cloud your judgment.

> *I'll just do the inspection myself and save the money.*
>
> *Let's just hire our trusted friend to inspect the home. He's a great handyperson.*
>
> *My brother is a licensed electrician. He can inspect the home and tell us what is wrong.*
>
> *We don't need an inspection. This is a brand-new home. The builder is first-rate.*
>
> *Our budget is so tight. Let's save the money now and worry about this later.*

Even the most experienced home seller or home buyer lacks the knowledge and expertise to conduct a professional home inspection. And because a home is where we raise children and where we gather with friends and family, buying a home has a huge emotional component. Even the most levelheaded buyer may find it difficult to remain objective and impartial when evaluating a home for deficiencies or maintenance issues.

A carpenter, handyperson, trade professional, friend, or family member is not a substitute for a professional home inspector. Contractors, carpenters, handypersons, electricians, and plumbers all play very important roles in home-building and home-improvement processes, and the really good ones are wonderful allies to homeowners. A home inspection should not be conducted by any of the following licensed or unlicensed professionals unless they have acquired the necessary training and have met home inspection credentialing, licensure, or certification requirements.

- General contractors
- Specialty contractors (electricians, plumbers, and HVAC technicians)
- Handypersons

General Contractors

A licensed general contractor has the required training and credentials to build or supervise the building of a structure. A general contractor is the quarterback and general manager of the construction crew. As the general manager, the general contractor hires all of the subcontractors, and as the quarterback, the general contractor calls the plays. Sometimes the coordination of tasks or the integration of systems can lead to deficiencies or potential issues. Even a newly constructed home by a highly reputable, extremely conscientious contractor can have a major deficiency.

The case of the faulty gutters is a great example. This was a new construction. To the naked eye, the gutters looked great, but to the trained eye of a professional home inspector, the gutters were not installed properly. Sure, the problem might not present itself after a rainstorm or two. But eventually, improperly installed or inadequately maintained gutters can cause water damage to the interior of the home.

The Faulty Gutters

If gutters are not installed properly or maintained properly, water can find its way inside the exterior walls of a home and cause water damage to drywall or molding.

Here's another real-world example.

$5 Plumber's Glue Solves a $5,000 Potential Problem

While inspecting a newly-constructed home, I discovered that the condensation line coming off of the air handler was not properly connected and was leaking onto the top of the furnace in the crawlspace. This was a simple oversight that in time could require thousands of dollars to repair or upward of $5,000 to replace the furnace.

The leaking condensation line would not become an immediate problem. It might take a year or several years for the problem to evolve into a costly issue requiring immediate attention. But one day, if the issue was left unchecked, the furnace would fail. And because the furnace was in the crawlspace, the issue might go unchecked until the furnace failed and the problem became costly.

The services and expertise of a general contractor and a home inspector are complementary, not interchangeable. There are times when a general contractor and a home inspector work closely together to ensure proper and safe construction of structures, as is the case during lender-required draw inspections (as described in the New Home and Draw Inspection section), but one is not a substitute for the other.

Specialty Contractors

A licensed, trade-specific contractor (such as an electrician, plumber, or HVAC technician) typically has extensive training and experience in their specific area of expertise. Obtaining a trade-specific license generally means that the person has completed a minimum number of hours as an apprentice, has passed a state-required exam, and is current on state-required continuing education hours. While specialty contractors are masters at their trade, they have not received any training, nor do they have credentials to perform a home inspection unless they have acquired home inspection training and passed a home inspection competency exam.

Handypersons

Unless specific home inspection training has been acquired, a handyperson is also not qualified to perform a home inspection. Handypersons are skillful repairers. Typically, they do not focus on the reason why a problem started or why a particular component failed. For example, let's say a window fails to open and close properly. The handyperson will repair the window and ensure that it opens and closes properly; the home inspector will tell you why the window failed in the first place. The home inspector might have to evaluate the integrity of the foundation of the structure from outside or underneath the home, but a thorough home inspector determines the cause of the deficiency, not how to fix it. Different skills and different perspectives translate into different people for different jobs.

Why Have a Home Inspected?

The home buying market first became aware of the need for property inspections back in the 1950s. In the early 1970s home buyers began to hire general contractors to perform pre-purchase inspections on homes. The home inspection industry was born out of the 1984 landmark case *Easton v. Strassberger*. This California case held that realtors have

> "an affirmative duty to conduct a reasonably competent and diligent inspection of the residential property listed for sale and to disclose to prospective purchasers all facts materially affecting the value of the property that such investigation would reveal."[4]

In other words, the court case informed realtors that they had a due diligence to buyers to inspect and disclose deficiencies to the buyer before finalizing the sale. The real estate industry's response to the requirement that a home be inspected was to establish an arm's-length transaction with an objective, qualified third party: a professional home inspector.

According to a 2003 National Association of Realtors study, more than 82 percent of home buyers nationwide hired a professional home inspector before buying a home.[5] Current 2016 home buying practices suggest more than 90 percent of all homes

---

[4] "Easton v. Strassburger (1984)," accessed April 20, 2016, http://law.justia.com/cases/california/court-of-appeal/3d/152/90.html.
[5] National Association of REALTORS® Research Division, *The 2003 National Association of REALTORS® Survey of Real Estate Services* (Chicago, IL: National Association of REALTORS®, 2003), 1.

nationwide are inspected by a professional home inspector.

All homes should be inspected by a professional home inspector even if the structure is going to be demolished and the land used for another purpose. If you intend to demolish the structure, negotiate a limited home inspection with the home inspector. No sense having all of the structures and systems evaluated for deficiencies if the structures are going to be demolished. Tell the home inspector your intention for the property and ask the inspector to focus on land, safety, and environmental issues that might impact demolition and rebuilding on the lot.

Why are almost all homes nationwide inspected by a professional home inspector? Because the benefits of doing so are just too compelling not to. Here are the main reasons why home buyers and home sellers have homes inspected.

✓ **Make an Informed Decision**

A home inspection will help a home buyer make an informed purchase decision or help a home seller determine an appropriate selling price. Having a home inspected when buying a home is analogous to getting the CARFAX®

when buying a car. Know the facts about a home's condition before buying it—before making a huge investment in a property.

- ✓ **Discover Deficiencies and Maintenance Issues Before Buying**

  Many real estate contracts describe the home as being sold in "as is" condition. Knowing the deficiencies of a property up front helps the buyer understand what "as is" condition means for a given property and helps the buyer better assess the true value of the property.

- ✓ **Discover Deficiencies and Maintenance Issue Before Selling**

  Sellers who have a pre-sale home inspection completed are often ahead of the game as compared to other sellers who have not. Sellers who provide pre-sale inspections and repair receipts send a message to potential buyers that they are serious and transparent about selling their home. The other advantage of offering a pre-sale inspection with repair receipts is to streamline the process and shorten the offer-to-close timeframe of a home purchase transaction.

- ✓ **Save Money at Closing**

  A home inspection is not a formality: it's an investment. A home inspection can save the buyer money at the closing. Fueled with information about deficiencies and the associated costs to remedy the deficiencies, the buyer has a powerful negotiation tool. Numbers don't lie, and numbers speak louder than words.

Missing Pipes

Foreclosure properties are notorious for being sold "as is" with little to no negotiation room on the price. After inspecting a foreclosure property that had been left vacant for some time, I discovered that all the copper pipes in the crawlspace had been removed. In this case due to the magnitude of the issue, the buyer was able to negotiate a significant reduction in the selling price of the property.

- ✓ **Become Aware of Safety or Environmental Issues**

  Safety and environmental issues can be deal-breakers in a real estate transaction for both buyer and lender reasons. The presence of toxic mold, asbestos, or WDOs might make a dream home suddenly look like a bad idea. A failing septic system can have a huge safety and environmental impact.

Septic Tank Troubles
Septic tank are not included in a routine home inspection, but a good home inspector can identify the early warning signs when one is starting to fail or has not been maintained properly.

✓ **Reduce Risk**

The ultimate purpose for having a home inspected is to reduce the financial risk of buying a home. But having a home inspected cannot and does not reduce all the risk. It is important to keep in mind these two very important tenets.

- A home inspection is NOT a risk-free determination.
- A home inspection is NOT a pass-fail test.

Homes age, systems wear out, and sometimes the rules change. A home does not pass or fail a home inspection. The life of a home is a moving target, and a home inspection is a visual inspection at a specific point in time. So while squeaky floorboards might seem charming to the owner who has gotten used to them over time, they could also be early warning signs of a foundation that is failing.

Squeaky Floors

It is not uncommon for floors to squeak in an older home, but a good home inspector knows the difference between old, squeaky floorboards and a foundation that is starting to fail.

Put Me In, Coach: Selecting the Right Home Inspector

Selecting the right home inspector is an important decision because selecting the wrong one can cost the home buyer money. It's like trying to win a game by having the quarterback kick a winning field goal. Quarterbacks and field goal kickers are both exceptional football athletes, but their skills are not interchangeable. Training, certification, licensure, and experience all matter when selecting the right home inspector.

Checklist for Selecting the Right Home Inspector

When choosing a home inspector, look for a qualified, professional home inspector that has been licensed by the state and/or has obtained certification through a national home inspection organization. Adherence to standards of practice and a code of ethics plus compliance with a continuing education requirements are important factors when choosing a qualified, professional home inspector. Most of the states that require licensure have webpages that verify licensed home inspectors by geographic area.

This is a valuable resource that makes verifying licensure quick and easy.

Consider these important variables before selecting a professional home inspector.

- ✓ **Training and Education: Experience Matters**
  Before hiring a professional home inspector, take a moment to familiarize yourself with the licensing or certification requirements in your state, then verify that the home inspector meets these requirements. Does the home inspector proudly display compliance with licensure and membership in prestigious organizations on his or her website? Either way, be sure to ask. Even if you live in an unregulated state, it's a good idea to ask if the home inspector has voluntarily obtained certification.

  While professional training and compliance with state requirements are essential, professional experience matters more. Inspecting homes is a hands-on job, and states like Alabama, Connecticut, Delaware, and Texas regulate associate home inspection internships or training programs as a prerequisite for becoming an entry-level, state-licensed home inspector. In Alabama, a year of fieldwork is required.

A seasoned home inspector views a home from a home building and home maintenance perspective. Does the home inspector have experience in any other home-related industry, like construction or real estate? Ask the home inspector about years of experience inspecting homes, and ask if the inspector is certified or experienced in any specialty areas of home inspection—know who you are hiring.

✓ **References and Reputation**

For states that regulate home inspectors, state laws include good-moral-character clauses and specify business practices and consequences for criminal actions. Many states prohibit licensure based on a record of criminal activity. Currently, nine states require the submission of fingerprints for the purpose of conducting a criminal background check.

A good way to find a professional home inspector is to ask friends and family members for a referral. In many states, real estate agents are legally prohibited from recommending just one home inspector because of potential conflict of interest issues or failure to maintain an arm's-length transaction. If a friend or family member had a good experience with a home inspector, chances are you will too. But don't rely solely on a good referral; be sure to ask the important questions and always ask for and verify references.

✓ **Liability Insurance**

Many states now require that professional home inspectors carry a minimum amount of liability insurance. Across the states that have a liability-insurance requirement, the amount varies from $20,000 to $500,000, and four states also require that a home inspector be bonded. Even if you live in a state that does not require liability insurance, it is still a good idea to ask if the home inspector voluntarily carries liability insurance.

✓ **Home Inspection Report**

Many states have detailed written and oral reporting requirements for home inspectors. A couple of states like Texas and Louisiana even require that the home inspector pass a specific report-writing course. Clear communication of the findings by a professional home inspector is critical if the home buyer or home seller is to benefit from the investment of having a home inspection conducted. Here are some key issues to ask concerning the home inspection report.

- Does the written report include pictures of deficiencies?
- Does the written report include a written description of major deficiencies, not just a checked box?
- How many pictures are typically included in the final report?
- Is there a preliminary oral report of major deficiencies?
- When will the final report be available?
- Can the final report be amended if something is not clear in the report?

- ✓ **Value-Added Services**

  Besides a full, detailed report with explanations of deficiencies and areas of concern with pictures, a thorough home inspector also evaluates structures and systems that are not routinely included in a home inspection. State licensing and standards of practice guidelines outline what is and is not routinely evaluated in a home inspection. Even though ASHI Standards of Practice for home inspectors may not include evaluation of the following systems and structures, some inspectors do so as a courtesy if state law does not specifically prohibit such action:

  - Fences
  - Septic tanks
  - Detached structures like sheds
  - Smoke and carbon monoxide alarms
  - Swimming pools

  As a courtesy, does the home inspector include any services that are not typically included in a home inspection or are excluded by ASHI Standards of Practice?

✓ **Home Inspection Warranty**

A home inspection evaluation is typically not warrantied: a professional home inspector does not guarantee the condition of the structure or system evaluated. A home inspection evaluation is the opinion of a professional home inspector after a visual examination at a moment in time. Some home inspectors do, however, offer a limited home inspection warranty.

A home inspection warranty is not the same as a home warranty, and here's the difference. A home warranty is an insurance-type contract purchased by a home seller or real estate agent from a home warranty company that serves as a peace-of-mind incentive to a home buyer. A home warranty is usually limited in duration to one year and provides repair and replacement services for appliances and major systems.

A home inspection warranty, on the other hand, is a service contract that covers mechanical and structural deficiencies not addressed by the home inspector in the home inspection report. Since a home inspection is a visual examination of a property at a point in time, the duration and scope of a home inspection warranty is usually very limited. A home inspection warranty typically expires within 90 days from the inspection date or a certain number of days after the closing whichever is sooner.

Both types of plans have exclusions and limitations. So for either type of plan, ask questions about what's covered and if there are any out-of-pocket expenses. While a home seller may offer a home warranty to make purchasing a home more attractive, a home inspector offers a home inspection warranty because the inspector is confident about the quality of work and inspection provided.

✓ **Cost**

The last and final consideration when selecting a professional home inspector is and should be cost; cost should never be the determining factor. Home inspection pricing varies by the size and age of a home: larger and older homes take longer and cost more to inspect. Across home inspectors in a geographic area for a given size and age of home, home inspection fees will not vary greatly. The right home inspector might not be the cheapest, but the inspector should be cost competitive.

National Organizations & State Regulations

This section describes the leading national organizations and outlines current state regulatory requirements in the home inspection industry. Information about each organization was obtained from a review of each organization's website at the time of publication. The information contained herein is subject to change at the discretion of the organization. Please check each organization's website for the most current information.

This section also overviews the state regulatory requirements for professional home inspectors. Even though there are several well-established and highly regarded national organizations and associations, the home inspection industry is state driven. To assess the current trends in state regulations for professional home inspectors, an independent survey was conducted. Results of this survey, the 2016

Survey of State Regulations for Home Inspectors, are reprinted in this book with permission. Since state requirements vary greatly, always check the specific laws and administrative codes in your state for the most current regulatory requirements.

There is one organization that dominates the home inspection industry in the area of a national competency exam for home inspectors. There are three organizations that dominate in the area of home inspector certification. All three of the certification organizations provide training, education, standards of practice guidelines, and a code of ethics for home inspectors.

National Home Inspector Examination (NHIE)

The Examination Board of Professional Home Inspectors (EBPHI) is an independent, nonprofit corporation whose sole mission is to develop and administer a home inspector competency exam: no training, no marketing, no membership, just an exam. Established in 1999, EBPHI is a nonprofit, volunteer-based organization that administers the NHIE.[6]

According to the 2016 survey, 90 percent of regulated states accept the NHIE as a required test for state licensure or certification. While passing the NHIE appears to be the gold standard in the home inspection industry, some states accept alternative tests to NHIE for licensure or certification. Even though there is no formal connection, the American Society of Home Inspector's Standards of Practice, as outlined in a 900-page manual, are recognized as the premier resource in the industry for successful completion of the NHIE. There are only two states (Nevada and North Carolina) that require a state-specific competency exam for certification and licensure, respectively.

American Society of Home Inspectors (ASHI)

The American Society of Home Inspectors, a nonprofit professional association, was established by a group of home inspectors in 1976.

---

[6] "About Us," National Home Inspector Examination, accessed April 20, 2016, http://www.homeinspectionexam.org/about_us.phb.

ASHI offers training, certification, continuing education in a variety of areas, and membership. ASHI does not have its own competency exam. To become an ASHI-certified home inspector, the home inspector must pass the NHIE. Currently, there are four states (Connecticut, Kentucky, South Carolina, and Vermont) that require ASHI certification for licensure, and wo states require passing the NHIE and the ASHI Code of Ethics exam for licensure (Alabama and Arkansas).

To become an ASHI-certified home inspector, each member must:

(1) pass the National Home Inspector Examination (NHIE),
(2) pass the ASHI Standards of Practice and Code of Ethics exams, and
(3) perform 250 home inspections.[7]

International Association of Certified Home Inspectors (InterNACHI)

InterNACHI is an international membership organization that provides training, examination, and marketing services to home inspectors. To

[7] "ASHI Membership Categories and Requirements," American Society of Home Inspectors, accessed April 20, 2016, http://www.homeinspector.org/ASHI-membership-categories-and-requirements.

become an InterNACHI-certified home inspector, each member must:

(1) pass the InterNACHI inspector exam,
(2) complete the InterNACHI Code of Ethics course,
(3) complete the InterNACHI Standards of Practice course,
(4) sign an affidavit of compliance,
(5) meet a continuing education requirement of 24 hours per year, and
(6) re-pass the exam every three years.[8]

InterNACHI also has more than thirty specialty certifications such as mold, radon testing, infrared, septic systems, and home energy to name a few. While this organization's exam is not the industry's leading competency exam, three states honor InterNACHI membership as an alternative requirement to NHIE for state licensure.

National Association of Home Inspectors (NAHI)

The National Association of Home Inspectors is a nonprofit, member association that offers a

---

[8] "Home Inspector Certification Requirements," International Association of Certified Home Inspectors, accessed April 20, 2016, http://www.nachi.org/cpi-requirements.htm.

Certified Real Estate Inspector (CRI) program plus training, standards of practice, and a code of ethics for home inspectors. Currently, North Dakota and Vermont accept NAHI-CRI as an option for licensure. To become a NAHI-CRI, each member must:

(1) pass the NAHI CRI exam,
(2) inspect 250 homes, and
(3) meet a continuing education requirement of 16 hours per year.[9]

Currently, Kentucky and West Virginia accept NAHI membership as a requirement for licensure. To become a member of NAHI without the CRI designation, each member must:

(1) pass either the NHIE exam or the NAHI-CRI exam,
(2) inspect 100 homes, and
(3) meet a continuing education requirement of 16 hours per year.[10]

International Code Council (ICC)

Established in 1994, the ICC is a nonprofit membership association dedicated to the development of international building codes and

---

[9] "Levels of Membership," National Association of Home Inspectors, accessed April 20, 2016, http://www.membersnahi.site-ym.com.
[10] See note 9.

safety standards for public and private structures. The ICC has a long history of offering state-sanctioned, journeyperson, and master certification programs for plumbers, mechanical engineers, pipefitters, and electricians throughout the United States.[11] But this organization is not a leader in the home inspection industry.

Two unregulated states (California and Georgia) recognize the Commercial and Residential Building Inspector Certifications offered by ICC. Alaska has separate home inspection licensing requirements for new homes versus existing homes. To inspect new homes, Alaska requires four ICC exams for licensure, but for existing homes the NHIE is required.

State Regulation

The need for professional home inspectors did not emerge until the 1970s. In the 1980s and 1990s, states began to see a need for state regulation of the profession. To assess the current trends in state regulatory requirements for home

[11] "About ICC," International Code Council, accessed April 20, 2016, http://www.iccsafe.org/about-icc/overview/about-international-code-council.

inspectors, a survey was conducted. The survey was conducting in April 2016 by reviewing online state laws and administrative codes. The results of this survey are summarized in appendices A and B.

Appendix A, "Summary of 2016 Survey of State Regulations for Home Inspectors," categorizes the current regulatory status of each state for a professional home inspector: not regulated, licensure, or certification. For states that regulate home inspectors through licensure or certification, the state agency or regulation is also listed. Appendix B, "Summary of 2016 State Regulatory Requirements for Home Inspectors," outlines current trends in regulatory requirements for the thirty-three regulated states. This table shows the prevalence of certain regulatory requirements across regulated states.

Based on the 2016 survey, thirty-three states (67 percent) regulate home inspectors through licensure or certification, and seventeen states are unregulated. There are only five states that require certification instead of licensure: Arizona, Nevada, Pennsylvania, Virginia, and West

Virginia. For the five states requiring certification, Nevada requires a state-specific exam, and the other four states require NHIE.

In the unregulated states, anyone with a flashlight and a ladder can promote and sell services as a home inspector without any legal ramification. And three unregulated states rely upon voluntary membership in a home inspector association. State regulation holds professional home inspectors accountable and serves to protect home buyers and home sellers in several very important ways.

- Training, education, and verification of competency
- Professional liability and criminal background checks
- Standards of practice and code of ethics
- Reporting requirements

The need for training, education, and verification of competency for professional home inspectors is generally accepted. The NHIE is accepted by 90 percent of the regulated states, demonstrating a strong trend toward reliance on this organization for verification of competency in the home inspection industry. Of the regulated states, 91 percent (30 states) require annual or biennial renewal, and 73 percent (24 states) require 8–20 hours of continuing education per year.

Professional liability is also a growing trend in the home inspection industry for regulated states: 73 percent (24 states) require $50,000–$500,000, and four states also require a surety bond. Fair-dealing and criminal-conduct language is also prevalent in state statutes and administrative codes. Currently, 27 percent of the regulated states (9 states) require a criminal background check.

At the heart of the home inspection industry are standards of practice that serve the profession and a code of ethics that protects the public. ASHI and other organizations provide leadership in this regard. In the regulated states, six states accept ASHI certification as a condition of state compliance, and two other states require the NHIE plus passing ASHI's Code of Ethics exam as a condition of compliance. Almost all the other regulated states have language about ethical conduct and fair-dealing practices in state statutes or administrative codes.

Use the information in appendices A and B as a starting place for gathering information about regulatory requirements for home inspectors in your state. At a minimum, ask about licensure, certification, and liability insurance when hiring a professional home inspector.

Section 2: The Home Inspection Process

Playbook: Types of Home Inspections

There are several types of home inspections. A routine home inspection is broad and includes all of the main structures and systems of a home, and a specialty inspection is limited to specific structures or issues. Each inspection serves a different purpose, and limited or focused inspections are not sufficient to meet the needs and purpose of a routine home inspection. The following types of inspection are discussed here:

- Routine home inspection
- New home and draw inspection
- Structure-specific inspection
- Wood-destroying organism (WDO) inspection
- Insurance inspection
- Structural inspection
- Safety inspection
- Environmental inspection
    - Asbestos
    - Radon gas
    - Lead
    - Mold and moisture

Routine Home Inspection

A routine home inspection is a visual examination of the condition of a home at a certain point in time, and the scope of structures and systems evaluated are defined by the standards of practice. ASHI Standards of Practice are the gold standard in the home inspection industry, but many states have adopted a hybrid or modified version of the ASHI Standards of Practice. An overview of the ASHI Standards of Practice for home inspection effective March 1, 2014, is outlined in this section. Use the information in this section as a benchmark. Be sure to ask the home inspector about specific structures and systems that are important to you, which may be excluded or included by statute in your state.

ASHI Standards of Practice include the following:

- Structure
- Exterior
- Roof
- Plumbing
- Electrical
- Heating and air conditioning
- Interior
- Insulation and ventilation
- Fireplaces and fuel-burning appliances

ASHI Standards of Practice specifically exclude the following structures and systems:

- Pools and spas
- Detached structures (except garages and carports)
- Outdoor kitchen appliances
- Landscape and irrigation systems
- Wells, well pumps, and water storage–related equipment
- Water conditioning systems
- Solar, geothermal, and other renewable energy water heating systems
- Manual and automatic fire-extinguishing and sprinkler systems
- Landscape irrigation systems
- Septic and other sewage disposal systems

ASHI Standards of Practice also specify that a home inspector is not required to determine:

- The condition of systems and components that are not readily accessible
- The remaining life expectancy of systems and components
- The strength, adequacy, effectiveness, and efficiency of systems and components
- The causes of conditions and deficiencies
- Methods, materials, and costs to repair or correct deficiencies

- The presence of plants, animals, and other life forms and substances that may be hazardous or harmful to humans including, but not limited to, wood destroying organisms, molds, and mold-like substances

Some of the above ASHI Standards are discretionary to a home inspector and other standards are strictly prohibited by state laws. So if a particular structure or system is of concern or importance to you, be sure to ask the home inspector about his or her standards of practice and scope of service.

Structural

The structural components of a routine home inspection include the foundation, crawlspace, attic, and roof. The interior walls, floors, and ceiling are also evaluated in a routine home inspection.

Wet Crawlspace: Never a Good Idea

It is never acceptable to have standing water or moisture in a crawlspace, not even during a rainy season or after a heavy downpour. Water or moisture in the crawlspace is a sign of trouble for two reasons: (1) the water is coming from somewhere, and (2) water, moisture, and oxygen are a recipe for pest infestation.

A good home inspector runs water in the home before inspecting the crawlspace to isolate internal sources of water leakage and evaluates the grade of the lot for potential drainage issues.

A home inspector is not required to offer an opinion about the adequacy of the structural systems and components or to provide an engineering or architectural analysis. ASHI Standards specify that the crawlspace should have at least 24 inches of vertical clearance and the access opening should be at least 18 inches in diameter.

Exterior

The exterior components of a routine home inspection include the exterior wall covering, flashing, trim, windows, and exterior doors of a home. Attached and adjacent decks, balconies, stoops, porches, and their associated steps and railings are also included in a routine home inspection. Eaves, soffits, and fasciae are evaluated from the ground level. Vegetation, grading, drainage, and retaining walls are only evaluated for impact upon the home structure, not as a primary source of deficiency.

Landscaping Matters

While landscaping and irrigation systems are outside the scope of a routine home inspection, trees and shrubs can cause deficiencies to a home. A good home inspector documents a deficiency when tree branches infringe upon the integrity of the roof and when shrubs are not at least 12 inches away from the exterior of a home.

A home inspector is not required to inspect screening, shutters, awnings, and similar seasonal accessories. Fences, boundary walls, pools, spas, and outbuildings other than garages and carports are also excluded from a routine home inspection.

Roof

The life expectancy of an asphalt-shingled roof is 18–25 years. The roof components of a routine home inspection include roofing material, the roof drainage system, flashing, skylights, and the chimney. A home inspector is not required to inspect antennas or the interiors of vents, flues, and chimneys that are not readily accessible.

Swaying, Warped, or Sagging Roof

A roof is a big-ticket item on a home. Know the condition of the roof before you buy. A swaying, warped, or sagging roof can be a sign that the integrity of the roofing system has been breached or it may be a sign of normal aging. A good home inspector knows how to tell the difference by looking in the attic and evaluating the entire roofing system for deficiencies.

Under certain conditions, a home inspector is not required to walk the roof to inspect it, but at minimum, a home inspector must inspect the roof from an eaves view using a 12-foot ladder.

Plumbing

The plumbing components of a routine home inspection include: (1) the interior water supply and distribution systems including fixtures and faucets, (2) the interior drain, waste, and vent systems including fixtures, (3) the water heating equipment and hot water supply system, and (4) sewage ejectors, sump pumps, and related piping.

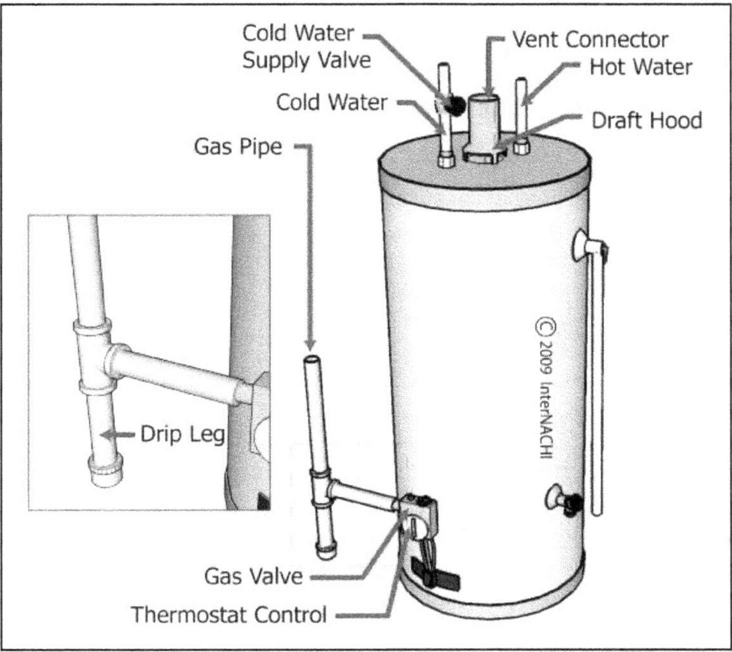

Figure 1: Illustration of a drip leg. Courtesy of the International Association of Certified Home Inspectors (InterNACHI)

According to ASHI Standards of Practice, a drip leg is required on a gas water heater and a gas furnace. A drip leg is a safety feature that catches and prevents sediment from flowing into a gas water heater or a gas furnace. Sediment in a gas water heater or furnace can block gas flow into the unit; a gas blockage can potentially cause an explosion.

Drip Legs: Standards and Codes Make Safety the Priority

I was told by a home builder of a half-million-dollar, custom home that a drip leg was not required by Arkansas building code. While home inspectors don't evaluate building code requirements, standards of practice for home inspectors do stipulate that a drip leg is required on a gas water heater or a gas furnace for safety reasons. After contacting the Arkansas-state plumbing inspector, I was informed that a drip leg is required under Arkansas building code and was provided a copy of the documentation. The home buyer was pleased that I did not take the builder's word and that I followed up with documentation. The builder corrected the deficiencies, and drip legs were added to the appliances.

A home inspector is not required to inspect any of the following plumbing-related systems:

- Washing machine connections
- Wells, well pumps, and water storage–related equipment
- Water conditioning systems
- Solar, geothermal, and other renewable energy water heating systems
- Manual and automatic fire extinguishing and sprinkler systems
- Landscape irrigation systems
- Septic and other sewage disposal systems

Electrical

The electrical components of a routine home inspection include service conductors, cables, raceways, and the main disconnects. Electrical service grounding and service drop clearances are also evaluated. Figure 2 shows the required electrical service drop clearances for homes in the United States.

Electrical service panels, subpanels, conductors, and overcurrent protection devices are also included, and the location of main disconnects and subpanels should be noted in the report. A

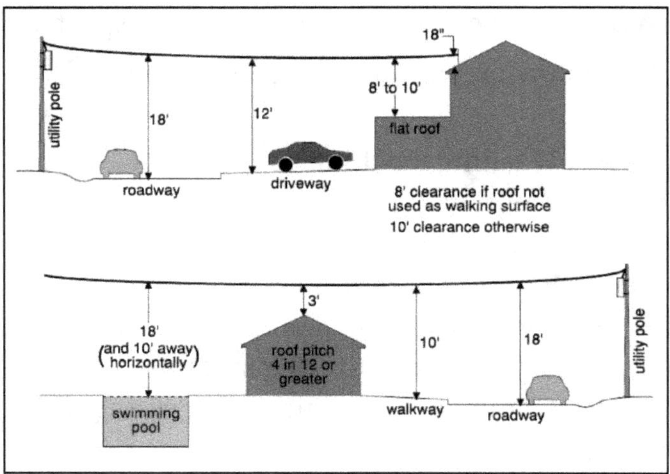

Figure 2: Diagram of service drop clearances. Courtesy of Carson Dunlop

home inspector is expected to test a representative number of installed lighting fixtures, switches, receptacles, and ground-fault circuit interrupters (GFCI) and arc-fault circuit interrupters (AFCI). While a home inspector is not expected to test smoke detectors or carbon monoxide alarms, an inspector is expected to note the presence or absence of them.

GFCIs Are Required

Ground-fault circuit interrupters (GFCIs) are required electrical outlets in kitchens, bathroom, home exteriors, and garages. A good home inspector not only identifies that they are properly placed throughout the home, but the inspector also makes sure that they all work properly.

Fuses and circuit breakers protect a home's electrical system from overloading circuits, overheating, and causing a potential fire. While circuit breakers are the most common form of overload protection found in new and updated homes, many older homes still have functioning fuse-based electrical panels. Local and municipal ordinances get updated over time. The fuses versus circuit breaker issue is a prime example of how an electrical system might have passed city ordinances when the home was purchased but fails revised ordinances when the owner goes to sell the property some years later.

A double-tapped circuit breaker—two wires connected to one breaker—is a safety issue if the breaker was not designed for two conductors. The presence of double-tapped circuit breakers might mean (1) the electrical service panel is reaching or exceeding its useful capacity, requiring an upgrade, or (2) the capacity is adequate but the breakers require an adjustment by an electrician; a good professional home inspector will know the difference. (See Figure 3 on next page.)

Fuses Versus Circuit Breakers

Discovering fuses in an electrical panel doesn't mean that there is a safety issue or that the fuses automatically need to be replaced with circuit breakers. But a double-tapped breaker could be a sign that the electrical system is overstressed and inadequate to meet the current electrical needs of the home.

A home inspector is not required to inspect remote control devices, low voltage wiring systems, or ancillary wiring systems. A home inspector is not expected to test security systems, smoke detectors, or carbon monoxide alarms. Solar, geothermal, wind, and other renewable energy systems are also outside the scope of a routine home inspection. A home inspector

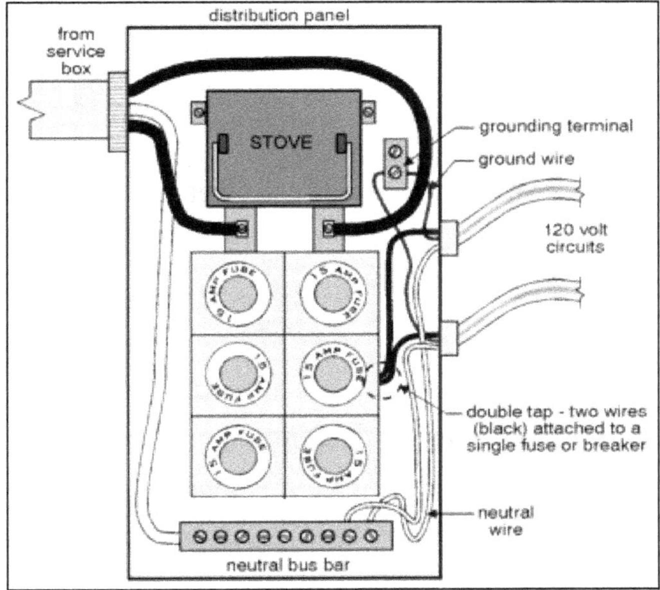

Figure 3: Image of a double-tapped fuse box

reports amperage, voltage, or impedance as part of a routine home inspection.

Heating and Air Conditioning

The heating and cooling components of a routine home inspection include a description and inspection of permanently installed equipment, vent systems, and distribution systems. A home inspector is expected to open and inspect readily openable access panels. The outside temperature should be above 65 degrees before turning on the air conditioning unit. If the outside temperature is below 65 degrees, the air conditioning unit may not be tested, but this information should be noted in the report.

A home inspector is not required to inspect heat exchanges, humidifiers, electric air cleaning devices, or whole-house mechanical ventilation systems (attic fans). Heating or cooling systems using ground-source, water-source, solar, or renewable energy technologies are also not included in a routine home inspection. A home inspector is not required to inspect a heating or cooling system that is installed in a window, but a home inspector is expected to inspect one that is installed in a wall.

Interior

The interior components of a routine home inspection include walls, ceilings, floors, steps, stairways, and railings. A representative number of installed cabinets, doors, and windows are also evaluated. Using normal operating controls, a home inspector is expected to test the primary function of garage door openers and installed appliances like ovens, ranges, cooktops, microwave ovens, dishwashers, and garbage disposals. A home inspector tests whether or not an installed appliance works, not necessarily how well it works (i.e., all the features or functions are not tested).

Sticking Doors

It is not uncommon for a door or window to stick especially in an older home. Sometimes homeowners overlook a charming nuance like a sticking door or a temperamental window. But a good home inspector knows the difference between a charming nuance that just needs an adjustment versus one that suggests a potential structural issue.

A home inspector is not required to inspect paint, wallpaper, floor coverings, window treatments, countertops, and other finish treatments. Central vacuum systems are not included in a routine home inspection. Installed, free-standing kitchen and laundry appliances like washers, dryers, refrigerators, and microwave ovens are not included in a routine home inspection.

Insulation and Ventilation

The insulation and ventilation components of a routine home inspection include insulation and

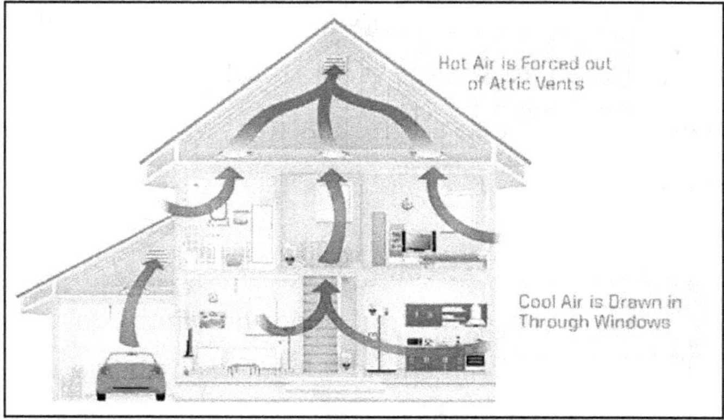

Figure 4: Diagram of a home ventilation system

vapor retarders in unfinished spaces, and ventilation of attics and foundations. Figure 4 demonstrates how a home's ventilation system facilitates the movement of fresh air through a home.

Inspections of clothes dryers, kitchens, bathrooms, and laundry exhaust systems are also included in a routine home inspection. A home inspector is expected to note the absence of insulation in unfinished spaces, but a home inspector is not required to disturb insulation to inspect it.

Who Cares About Compressed Insulation?

Insulation in an attic should be at least 8 inches thick and cover all the living areas in the home. Insulation can become compressed over time, and insulation standards have evolved over the years to help make homes more energy efficient. A good home inspector measures the thickness of insulation to ensure compliance with minimum standards.

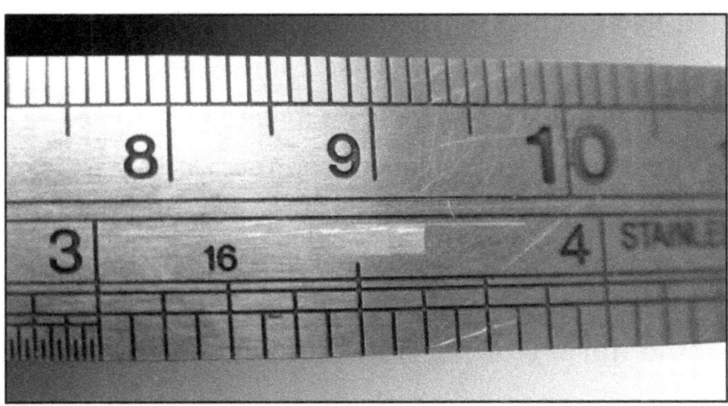

Here's another real-life example.

Oops, Who Needs Insulation? Everyone

All homes require insulation. On more than one occasion, I have been asked to inspect a new home and have discovered no insulation in the home.

Fireplaces and Fuel-Burning Appliances

The components of fireplaces and fuel-burning appliances evaluated in a routine home inspection include fuel-burning fireplaces, stoves, fireplace inserts, and installed fuel-burning accessories. Proper working order of chimneys and vent systems are also evaluated.

> **Fireplace Safety: Fire Walls and Flues**
>
> A fireplace can be a wonderful accessory in a home. A home inspector evaluates a fireplace through the lens of safety, not cosmetics. A good home inspector looks for all combustible materials like insulation, and roof decking to be at least 1 ½ inches from metal flues, and the presence of fire-resistant walls as required.

A home inspector is not required to inspect the interior of vent systems, flues, and chimneys that are not readily accessible. Mantels and fireplace surrounds, fireplace screens, doors, seals and gaskets, or automatic fuel-feed devices are not included in a routine home inspection. Determining draft characteristics is also not part of a routine home inspection. Pilot lights are not lit, and shut-off valves are outside the scope of a home inspection.

New Home and Draw Inspection

New homes can undergo a full or phased inspection. A home buyer might order a full inspection on a newly constructed home, and a lender or warranty company might require a phased inspection on a new construction project. While the timing of these two different types of new home inspections may vary, the standards of practice are identical to a routine home inspection.

A phased inspection ordered by a lender or warranty company is also called a draw inspection. The purpose of a draw inspection is to ensure that certain standards are met at specific construction milestones. The name *draw inspection* is derived from the fact that the contractor draws money from the lender after certain phases of construction are successfully completed. There are three phases to a draw inspection: foundation, framing, and final. At the completion of each phase of construction, a home inspector is called in to inspect the home and issue an all-clear report for that phase of construction, and the home inspector's all-clear report signals release of funds from the lender. This is a great example of how contractors and home inspectors work closely together.

A home buyer purchasing a newly constructed home that has not been previously inspected should have the home inspected by a professional home inspector: no if, ands, or buts. Even a home built by a highly reputable, conscientious contractor should be inspected for deficiencies.

Don't make the mistake of thinking that building inspectors have fully evaluated the structures and systems of a newly constructed home. Municipal and state building code departments review plans, issue permits, and perform inspections to ensure compliance with regulated building codes; they do not perform a visual inspection of the working structures and systems of a home. Contractors and building code inspectors are state-licensed professionals who are schooled in building code requirements, not in home inspection standards and practices.

Structure-Specific Inspection

Some accessory structures and integral systems are not covered under the scope of a routine home inspection. Structures or systems like pools and spas or septic systems are examples. Evaluation of these structures and systems requires specialized training and experience. InterNACHI and ASHI both offer continuing-education courses in the areas of septic system inspection and pool and spa inspections.

Wood-Destroying Organism Inspection

A wood-destroying organism (WDO) inspection, commonly referred to as a termite inspection, looks for past or current evidence of infestation by wood-devouring or wood-destroying organisms like termites and beetles. A WDO inspection also looks for evidence of past treatments or conditions conducive to infestations. While termite infestation is moderate to heavy across the entire lower half of the continental United States, termite infestation is very high in California and the southeastern Gulf and Atlantic states from Texas to Florida and up the coast to the Carolinas. Many lenders and mortgage companies in high-incident states require a WDO inspection or a WDO clearance letter for financing.

Insurance Inspection

An insurance inspection is also called a four-point inspection. Insurance companies sometimes require an inspection of a home's roof and electrical, plumbing, and HVAC systems. Because of the limited scope to these four areas, an insurance inspection is not a substitute for a comprehensive home inspection. ASHI offers a 3-hour course that is recognized by insurance companies in the state of Florida.

Structural Inspection

While an experienced home inspector can see signs and symptoms of structural issues, evaluating the structural integrity of a foundation is beyond the scope of a professional home inspector. If a home inspector suspects that there might be a structural issue with a home, it is prudent to have a structural inspection performed. A structural inspection is a visual examination of the physical structure (from attic to foundation) of a home by a specially trained and/or credentialed professional. In many instances, a structural inspector is an engineer.

Environmental Inspection

Environmental hazards in a home can involve air, surface, soil, or water contamination. Asbestos, radon gas, lead, and mold are the primary environment-based hazards that affect homes. While assessment of these four environmental hazards is beyond the scope of a routine home inspection, an experienced home inspector is your first line of defense for determining if an environmental inspection is necessary. Some home inspectors have the required additional training and credentials to perform an environmental inspection. The training programs for these specialized areas of expertise offered by ASHI and InterNACHI are 2–4 day seminars that also require passing an exam. Realtors are a great resource for identifying environmental issues and evaluating the need for testing and remediation.

Asbestos

Asbestos exposure is a known cause of serious respiratory disease including mesothelioma. Homes built between 1930 and 1950 commonly had asbestos installed for insulation. In the 1970s, the health risks of asbestos became widely known, and asbestos's widespread use was curtailed but not banned. Asbestos is still routinely used in gaskets, roofing materials, fireproofing materials, and hundreds of consumer goods used every day throughout the United States.

Asbestos scares everyone! If you suspect that the home may contain asbestos insulation, have an experienced asbestos assessment and abatement professional evaluate the situation.

Radon Gas

Radon is a colorless, tasteless, odorless, cancer-causing radioactive gas. Radon, a naturally occurring gas produced from uranium, can contaminate rock, soil, or well water in or around a home. If radon is present, it can slowly accumulate in a home over time. According to the Environmental Protection Agency (EPA) website, radon causes more than 21,000 lung cancer deaths nationwide every year and 80 percent of homes in the United States have never been tested. While the EPA has identified the mid-Atlantic, upper west, and upper Midwest region as a high-radon areas of the country, homes with elevated radon levels have been found in every state across the country. The EPA recommends purchasing a radon-testing kit at a hardware store to test for the presence of radon in a home. If radon is detected, then the EPA recommends hiring a National Radon

Proficiency Program (NRPP) certified professional.[12]

Lead

Like radon gas, lead is a naturally occurring element in the earth's crust. Unlike radon gas, most of the lead found in the environment comes from human activities and industrial sources. Familiar past and present products that contain lead and lead-based compounds include paint, ceramics, pipes, plumbing materials, solders, gasoline, batteries, ammunition, and cosmetics.

In 1978, the federal government banned the use of lead-based paint. According to the EPA website, millions of homes still contain lead-based paint and homes built before 1940 and homes built from 1940 to 1959 are 87 percent and 69 percent more likely to contain lead-based paint, respectively. The EPA further advises that deteriorating (i.e., chipping,

[12] "Health Risk of Radon," United States Environmental Protection Agency, accessed April 20, 2016, http://www.epa.gov/radon/health-risk-radon.

peeling, cracking) lead-based paint is hazardous requiring immediate attention. Evaluating the presence of or removing lead-based paint requires special training and certification.[13]

The EPA is responsible for administering the nation's lead-based paint abatement program. Beginning in April 2010, anyone performing renovation, repair, and painting projects that disturb lead-based paint in homes, child care facilities, and schools built before 1978 must be certified and must follow specific work practices to prevent lead contamination. Currently, there are 44 EPA-authorized training centers across the United States. If you suspect lead-based paint is present in a home, hire an EPA-trained, lead-based-paint inspector or abatement specialist.

---

[13] "Protect Your Family from Exposure to Lead," United States Environmental Protection Agency, accessed April 20, 2016, http://www.epa.gov/lead/protect-your-family-exposures-lead#sl-home.

Mold and Moisture

Mold and moisture can cause structural issues in homes and health issues in humans. Molds excrete toxic compounds called mycotoxins. Certain mycotoxins can be harmful or lethal to humans and animals when exposure is sufficiently high. Several states regulate mold inspectors or mold remediation professionals by requiring licensure or certification. If toxic mold is suspected, hire a trained mold inspection professional.

Preparation and Helpful Tips

The purposes of having a home inspected are to ascertain the structural and mechanical condition and to identify safety issues of a home at a point in time. Getting the most from the investment requires active participation in all three phases of the process: pre-inspection, inspection, and post-inspection. This section outlines three important time-sensitive tasks:

Prequalify a Home Inspector

Like prequalifying for a mortgage, it is helpful to prequalify a home inspector before you make an offer on a home. Screening and interviewing a home inspector before making an offer on a home will save precious time once the right home is selected and an offer is made.

Prepare and Submit a Repair Addendum

Once an offer is accepted, the buyer typically has 10–14 days to have the property inspected and submit a repair addendum. Because of this rather tight timeframe, having a home inspector lined up and ready to go is a huge timesaver.

Quantify and Prioritize Deficiencies

As outlined in the prior section, the scope of a home inspection is very clearly defined by state laws and standards of practice. To fully understand the condition of a property, sometimes specialty inspections or the advice and counsel of other home-industry professionals is necessary. If major deficiencies are discovered by a home inspector or if issues outside of the scope of a routine home inspection are suspected, other licensed or certified home-industry professionals like a specialty inspector, a contractor, an electrician, a plumber, a roofer, or a handyperson may be necessary. When this extra step is required, it is incumbent upon the home buyer to have all of this work completed within the same 10–14 day timeframe.

Section 3: The Home Inspection & the Home Inspection Report

Game Day: Inspection-Day Considerations

The most important decision, after selecting the right home inspector, is to attend the inspection. There are two reasons why attending the inspection is so valuable: (1) you get to ask questions and learn firsthand about the condition of the home and identified deficiencies, and (2) you get to observe the inspection process. So regardless of whether you are a home buyer having a home inspected or a homeowner having a pre-sale inspection completed, attend the inspection. Attending the inspection is an opportunity to participate in a one-on-one course in homeownership with a professional home inspector as your teacher. Every home buyer and homeowner should take advantage of the opportunity.

Three conditions that might cause a home inspection to be rescheduled are (1) the presence of wildlife, (2) excessive rain, or (3) the inactive status of utilities at time of the inspection. The presence of wildlife in an attic or crawlspace will cause a home inspection to be rescheduled. No home inspector is expected to work when raccoons, birds, or other wildlife are nesting or when nesting is suspected. The home buyer should ascertain if wildlife are present and resolve the matter with certainty before scheduling a home inspection.

Excessive rain can also delay or postpone a home inspection, especially if the home buyer prefers that the home inspector walk on the roof to inspect it. Excessive rain may create a safety issue for walking on the roof, but on the other hand, grading and lot drainage are better evaluated during or right after a period of excessive rain. The home buyer should assess the advantages and disadvantages of having a home inspected during excessive rain.

The home buyer should make sure that the utilities (gas, water, and electric) are turned on in the home at the time of the home inspection. Having the utilities turned on allows the home inspector to properly test and evaluate the heating, plumbing, and electrical systems and the installed appliances.

While it is important that both home buyers and home sellers attend the inspection, ask questions, and observe the process, this section outlines inspection-day considerations from the home buyer's perspective. (Note that it's best if the seller is not present for a home buyer's inspection.)

✓ **Attend the Inspection**

The importance of attending the inspection cannot be overstated. A thorough home inspection for a 2,000-square-foot home takes about 2 hours, and a larger home might take up to an additional hour to inspect. The biggest factor that affects the time it takes to inspect a home is the age of the home. Older homes take longer to inspect, and a very old home, like a hundred-year-old home, might take twice as long to inspect.

A good home inspector requires that the home buyer attend the home inspection. Before the home inspection begins, a professional home inspector should review the service contract and the scope of work for the inspection. The home inspector should review what is and is not covered for this particular home.

Ask the home inspector for an estimate of how long the home inspection will take, and be sure to allow enough time to ask questions after the inspection has been completed. Ask the inspector to notify you immediately if a major deficiency or major maintenance issue is identified. Tell the home inspector that you would like to see these issues firsthand.

Firsthand Experience Beats Secondhand Information Every Time

If you observe the process and the inspection report states that something was not inspected because the area was inaccessible, you will know firsthand how and why the area was inaccessible because you were there.

Safety concerns are a major reason why a good home inspector requires clients to attend the home inspection. Even though ASHI Standards exclude testing of smoke and carbon monoxide detectors, a good home inspector will point out the proper location of these important detectors. And a good home inspector will point out the location of shut-off valves and service connections for utilities in case of an emergency: valuable information to know in a critical situation when time is of the essence.

Don't Be Among the 70 Percent Who Are Unprotected

Approximately 70 percent of the homes I inspect don't have a carbon monoxide detector. If a home has an attached garage or a gas appliance, it needs a carbon monoxide detector.

✓ **Ask Questions**

Do a thorough walk-through of the home before the home inspection, and make a list of questions or concerns about anything that looks, smells, or feels unusual: use all of your senses, including the sense of intuition, to create your list of questions or concerns. No matter how slight or apparently silly the question may seem, bring all your questions or concerns to the home inspector's attention before the inspection. Confer with your realtor: ask your realtor if there was anything amiss that should be brought to the home inspector's attention. If at the end of the inspection, the home inspector doesn't know the answer to a question, ask the inspector to research the issue and get back to you. Make sure that all of your questions get answered.

- ✓ **Observe the Process**

While it is important to attend the inspection, it is also important not to get in the home inspector's way. Expect the home inspector to walk around the property and inspect the roof, crawlspace, and attic.

Besides expecting the home inspector to be on time, courteous, and organized, a home buyer should also expect the home inspector to have the right equipment to do the job properly and thoroughly. The three essential tools of a professional home inspector are a flashlight, a screwdriver, and a ladder. No flashlight, send the inspector home. Other equipment that a professional home inspector should have available are disposable overalls, shoe covers, and dust masks for crawling around the attic or crawlspace. The home inspector should also make these health and safety items available to the home buyer in the event that the home buyer wants to see an issue or deficiency in the attic or crawlspace firsthand.

Roof

Walking on a roof is the best method for inspecting a roof. While it is customary for a home inspector to walk on a roof to inspect it, certain types of roofs and certain conditions prohibit a home inspector from doing so. Walking on the roof might be prohibitive if the home is more than two stories, if the roof has a steep pitch, or if the roof is composed of clay, wood, or metal. Arkansas statute specifies that roofs with a pitch less than 6:12 must be inspected by walking on them and roofs with a pitch of 6:12 or greater may be inspected by viewing them from eave level if eaves are safely accessible with a 12-foot ladder. Ask the home inspector if the roof will be inspected by

walking on the roof. Soon using drones will become the standard for inspecting roofs and other hard-to-visualize areas.

Pitch is the Slope of a Roof

The pitch of a roof is a ratio that measures the roof's steepness. In geometry terms, the roof's pitch is the slope of a triangle. The pitch of a roof is a standardized ratio of the rise expressed in inches in relationship to 12 inches of run. The illustration below demonstrates the relationship between the rise and the run of a roof with a 6:12 pitch.

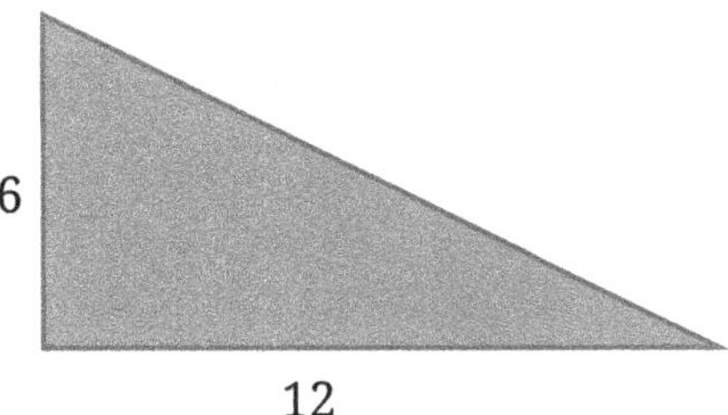

If the home inspector is unable to walk on the roof, the reason for not walking on the roof should be stated in the report. When walking on the roof is prohibited, the home inspector should provide observations about the condition of the roof from the eaves or from the ground by using a good set of binoculars. If major deficiencies or potential deficiencies are observed, the home inspector should recommend a roof inspection expert in the home inspection report.

Attic

The attic is included in a home inspection. Standards of practice stipulate that a home inspector should not disturb insulation or walk on rafters in an attic. Disturbing insulation or walking on insulation can decrease the R-value of the insulation, but the home inspector should carefully measure the depth of insulation in the attic and report this information in the inspection report.

Crawlspace

An inspector should inspect the crawlspace. For safety reasons, standards of practice stipulate that the access must be at least 18 inches in diameter and free from standing water and wildlife.

The presence of water in the crawlspace poses a potentially life-threatening hazard to a home inspector: water and electricity don't mix.

✓ **Get a Verbal Report**

At the end of the home inspection, ask the home inspector for a verbal report and take copious notes. The focus of the post-inspection conversation should be to clarify outstanding pre-inspection or inspection-revealing concerns. This is a short list of post-inspection questions to consider:

- What are some positive or favorable findings?
- Are there any safety issues?
- Are there any signs of environmental issues?
- What are the major deficiencies?

- Will the report include pictures of the major deficiencies?
- Does the home inspector recommend any specialty inspections?
- When will the home inspection report be available?
- What is the home inspector's policy and availability for follow-up questions?

While positive features or well-maintained components of a home's structures and systems are typically not reported in a home inspection report, understanding both positive and deficient features of a home's structures and systems will create a balanced perspective. There may be recently upgraded or extremely well-maintained systems or structures that were not fully appreciated or noticed on prior walk-throughs of the home. And starting off positive is always a great place to begin.

The most important question to ask is, are there any safety issues? Big or small, existing and potential safety issues of a home must be understood by the home buyer. It is the responsibility of a professional home inspector to identify and report all existing and potential safety issues, from latches on gates not working to the suspected presence of toxic material or a pest infestation.

After safety issues, the second most important question to ask is, are there any major deficiencies? Make a list, take thorough notes, and understand why each major issue is a deficiency and the cause of the deficiency. While ASHI Standards of Practice specifically state that a home inspector is not required to determine the cause of a deficiency, a good home inspector investigates each deficiency until the cause is determined.

Ask the home inspector to include pictures of all major deficiencies in the report, and ask the home inspector if any specialty inspections are recommended. Evaluating major deficiencies, acquiring repair bids, and having to schedule a specialty inspection are three significant events that could potentially delay the purchase transaction.

Ask the home inspector exactly when and how the inspection report will be available. Will the inspection report be available in both paper and electronic formats? Typically, an inspection report is available in 1–2 days. There are many software systems on the market for generating a home inspection report. Some inspection report software systems produce a check-off report in as little as 15–30 minutes, but a check-off report can be very limited. A proper report should contain a narrative description of each major deficiency. Pictures with graphics such as arrows or circles should also be provided to highlight or explain the deficiencies and issues.

Lastly, ask the home inspector about availability for follow-up questions or a follow-up inspection. Is the home inspector willing to discuss questions directly with a handyperson, a contractor, or the realtor? Is there a limited time that the home inspector will answer questions? What about after the closing? Will the home inspector still answer questions after the real estate transaction is complete? How amenable is the home inspector to re-inspecting deficiencies, and is there an extra charge?

Game Plan: Understanding and Benefiting from the Report

The primary purpose of having a home inspected is to ascertain the current condition of the home and then be able to use that information to decide if this is the right home at the right price for you. The inspection report is a powerful decision-making and negotiation tool. So even if a home buyer does not plan on requiring a home seller to resolve deficiencies, it is still prudent for the home buyer to be aware of deficiencies and associated costs to resolve them. Buying a new home and the prospect of moving into a new neighborhood is exciting. Don't let the excitement of the moment cloud the difficult business decision that lies ahead: buying the right home at the right price.

Taking a logical and structured approach to evaluating deficiencies will help to minimize the emotional component and maximize the value of the information in the home inspection report. Consider these four steps as preparation before meeting with the realtor to create a negotiation strategy.

Step 1: Read and understand the report

Step 2: List and quantify the major versus minor deficiencies

Step 3: Schedule specialty inspections or contractor evaluations

Step 4: Develop a strategy

✓ **Read the Report**

Read the home inspection report in detail, and ask for clarification from the home inspector if needed. Look at the pictures, and make sure you understand each deficiency, what is depicted in each picture, and what is required to resolve each deficiency. The home inspection report is the home buyer's tool for making an informed decision. Don't just hand the report to the realtor. If necessary, set up a three-way call between the home inspector, the realtor, and yourself to discuss the report. Whatever it takes, make sure you understand what's in the home inspection report.

✓ **Qualify and Quantify Deficiencies**

Not all deficiencies are of equal weight or importance. The home inspector's oral and written reports should differentiate between major and minor deficiencies. In practical terms, a major deficiency affects the habitability of the home or is costly to remedy. Draft a list of major versus minor deficiencies based on the home inspector's oral and written reports and your firsthand experience walking through and inspecting the home. In your mind, are there any potential deal killers? These "Red Flags" need to be reviewed from every angle.

Now it's time to meet with your realtor. Show the realtor your qualified list of major versus minor deficiencies and issues. Discuss each item on the list with your realtor, and jointly develop an action plan for assessing the financial impact of each deficiency or issue.

Schedule specialty inspections if they have been recommended by the realtor or the home inspector. Schedule contractors to evaluate deficiencies and estimate the costs to resolve them. In some cases, getting more than one cost bid may be prudent. Even if you do not plan on asking the home seller to resolve a deficiency, it's still very important to know what it costs to do so.

✓ **Develop a Strategy**

This is where a great realtor shines, and this is where a great realtor can save the home buyer money, sometimes a lot of money. Rely on the realtor for advice about what should and shouldn't be included in the repair addendum. Everything is negotiable, and the home inspection report coupled with cost estimates are the tools required to get the job done right. Make a list of Red Flags and associated price reductions, and know your bottom line.

Essentially, five negotiation strategies exist:

- Strategy 1: Ask that everything be resolved.
- Strategy 2: Ask for Red Flag deficiencies to be resolved.
- Strategy 3: Accept the property "as is."
- Strategy 4: Negotiate a price reduction.
- Strategy 5: Reject the sale and walk. Game over!

In the real world, few issues are black-and-white, and negotiating a real estate transaction is no exception. Oftentimes the final negotiation strategy is a combination of multiple strategies. While market conditions will have a big impact on which strategy or combination of strategies will work best, the sage advice of an experienced realtor is invaluable at this stage in a real estate transaction.

Two Minute Warning

Time to wrap up. This book is a how-to consumer's guide to the home inspection process and the home inspection industry. Filled with practical and easy-to-understand language, it breaks down and clarifies the home inspection process. It should be required reading for anyone who is about to buy or sell a home. This book educates home buyers and home sellers about the purpose and need for a home inspection, teaches them how to select the right home inspection partner, and helps them navigate through and benefit from the home inspection process and the home inspection report.

Three fundamental questions were answered in this book:

- What is a residential home inspection?
- Why have a home inspected?
- Why hire a professional home inspector?

A home inspection is an objective, visual examination of the readily accessible physical structures and installed systems of a home at a point in time. Knowing what a home inspection is and is not, understanding why and how to hire a professional home inspector, and benefiting from the home inspection report are important advantages when buying or selling a home.

Remember, the home buyer is like the owner of a football team; the home inspector and the realtor work for the home buyer. It is up to the home buyer to coordinate the activities of the players in the game of buying a home. Select your team players wisely, participate in the process, and use the home inspection report as a powerful negotiation tool.

Protect your assets by having the home you are considering buying inspected. The cost of a home inspection is a small price to pay in exchange for peace of mind and valuable information about the true condition of a property. Make sure you are acquiring the home of your dreams and not your worst nightmare.

Appendix A

Summary of 2016 Survey of State Regulations for Home Inspectors

Alabama	Licensure by Alabama Building Commission
Alaska	Licensure by Division of Business and Professional Licensing
Arizona	Certification
Arkansas	Licensure by Arkansas Home Inspection Registration Board
California	Not regulated by the state
Colorado	Not regulated by the state
Connecticut	Licensure by Home Inspection Licensing Board
Delaware	Licensure by Division of Professional Regulation, Board of Home Inspectors
Florida	Licensure by Florida Department of Business and Professional Regulation
Georgia	Not regulated by the state; voluntary

Hawaii	Not regulated by the state
Idaho	Not regulated by the state
Illinois	Licensure under Home Inspector License Act
Indiana	Licensure by Home Inspector Licensing Board
Iowa	Not regulated by the state
Kansas	Not regulated by the state, law expired in 2013
Kentucky	Licensure under Kentucky Home Inspector Licensing Law
Louisiana	Licensure by Louisiana State Board of Home Inspectors
Maine	Not regulated by the state; voluntary membership in MeChips
Maryland	Licensure by Department of Labor, Licensing, and Regulation
Massachusetts	Licensure under Board of Registration of Home Inspectors
Michigan	Not regulated by the state; voluntary
Minnesota	Not regulated by the state; some cities require licensure

Mississippi	Licensure by Mississippi Real Estate Commission
Missouri	Not regulated by the state
Montana	Not regulated by the state
Nebraska	Not regulated by the state
Nevada	State certified
New Hampshire	Licensure by Board of Home Inspectors
New Jersey	Licensure by Home Inspection Advisory Committee
New Mexico	Not regulated by the state
New York	Licensure under Home Inspector Professional License Law
North Carolina	License by North Carolina Home Inspection Licensure Board
North Dakota	Licensure under North Dakota Century Code Chapter 43-54
Ohio	Not regulated by the state
Oklahoma	Licensure under Oklahoma Home Inspection Licensing Act

Oregon	Licensure by Oregon Construction Contractors Board
Pennsylvania	Certification by a national home inspection association
Rhode Island	Licensure by Rhode Island Contractors' Registration Licensing Board
South Carolina	Licensure by South Carolina Residential Builders Commission
South Dakota	Licensure by South Dakota Real Estate Commission
Tennessee	Licensure under Home Inspection Licensing Program
Texas	Licensure by Texas Real Estate Licensing Board
Utah	Not regulated by the state
Vermont	Licensure under Office of Professional Regulation
Virginia	Certification by Virginia Board of Asbestos, Lead, and Home Inspectors
Washington	Licensure by Washington Department of Licensing
West Virginia	Certification by Office of the State Fire Marshall
Wisconsin	Licensure by Wisconsin Department of Safety and Professional Services

Wyoming	Not regulated by the state

Source: 2016 Survey of State Regulations for Home Inspectors

Appendix B

Summary of 2016 State Regulatory Requirements for Home Inspectors

Section 1

	Regulation	NHIE National Exam	ASHI Certification	InterNACHI Certification
Alabama	Licensure	Y	Ethics only	
Alaska	Licensure	Y		
Arizona	Certification	Y		
Arkansas	Licensure	Y	Ethics only	
Connecticut	Licensure	Y	Y	Y
Delaware	Licensure	Y		
Florida	Licensure	Y		Y
Illinois	Licensure	Y		
Indiana	Licensure	Y		
Kentucky	Licensure	Y	Y	Y

Louisiana	Licensure	Y		
Maryland	Licensure	Y		
Massachu-setts	Licensure	Y		
Mississippi	Licensure	Y		
Nevada	Certification			
New Hampshire	Licensure	Y		
New Jersey	Licensure	Y		
New York	Licensure	Y		
North Carolina	Licensure			
North Dakota	Licensure	Y	Y	Y
Oklahoma	Licensure	Y		
Oregon	Licensure	Y		
Pennsylvania	Certification	Y	Y	Y
Rhode Island	Licensure	Y		
South Carolina	Licensure	Y	Y	
South Dakota	Licensure	Y		

Tennessee	Licensure	Y		
Texas	Licensure	Y		
Vermont	Licensure	Y	Y	
Virginia	Certification	Y		
Washington	Licensure	Y		
West Virginia	Certification	Y		
Wisconsin	Licensure	Y		
TOTAL	**33**	**31**	**6**	**5**

Section 2

	Criminal Background Check	Liability Insurance	Surety Bond	Renewal	Cont. Ed. Hours
Alabama		Y		Annual	
Alaska	Y	Y	Y	Annual	Y
Arizona	Y	Y	Y		
Arkansas		Y		Annual	Y
Connecticut				Biennial	
Delaware		Y		Biennial	Y
Florida		Y		Biennial	Y
Illinois				Biennial	Y
Indiana	Y	Y		Biennial	Y
Kentucky		Y		Biennial	Y

Louisiana		Y		Annual	Y
Maryland		Y		Biennial	Y
Massachusetts		Y		Biennial	Y
Mississippi		Y		Biennial	Y
Nevada	Y	Y			
New Hampshire	Y			Biennial	Y
New Jersey	Y	Y		Biennial	Y
New York		Y		Biennial	Y
North Carolina		Y	Y	Annual	Y
North Dakota		Y		Annual	
Oklahoma		Y		Annual	Y
Oregon		Y	Y	Biennial	Y
Pennsylvania		Y			
Rhode Island		Y		Biennial	
South Carolina				Biennial	
South Dakota	Y			Biennial	Y

Tennessee		Y		Biennial	Y
Texas	Y	Y		Biennial	Y
Vermont				Biennial	
Virginia				Biennial	Y
Washington				Biennial	Y
West Virginia	Y			Annual	Y
Wisconsin		Y		Biennial	Y
TOTAL	**9**	**24**	**4**	**30**	**24**

Source: 2016 Survey of State Regulations for Home Inspectors

About the Author

Chris Perry is America's Home Inspection Referee.

Chris has successfully combined his passion for refereeing football with his passion for inspecting homes: his skills in one benefiting the other.

Chris, a native of Little Rock, Arkansas, first learned about a home-related industry while working alongside his father in the family construction business. Chris has also been in the home inspection business since 1996. He has worked as a termite inspector for a national company, as a building inspector for the city of Little Rock, and as a FEMA inspector post-Katrina.

Chris has even dabbled in the real estate industry. Chris's real estate experience helped him realize that his calling was not in selling homes but in evaluating the working systems and components of a home. When Chris views or enters a home his attention is drawn to the construction and maintenance of the home, not the cosmetics.

Likewise, when Chris walks on a football field to referee a game, his attention is drawn to the position and action of the players, not the color of their uniforms. Chris has been officiating youth and high school football since 2002. He is a member and past president of the Arkansas Officials Association, and he is founder of 5th & 1 Arkansas Referees.

Whether he is officiating a football game or crawling through an attic on a home inspection, Chris always dons a big, wide smile. His professional, courteous, and friendly demeanor has made him a highly respected member of the home inspection community. On or off the field, Chris is the type of person you want calling the shots.

The Official Guide to Home Inspections: Knowing and Playing by the Rules

Printed in the United States of America.

Chris Perry
501-960-4044
AmericasHomeInspectionReferee.com

ISBN-10: 0-9883878-5-9
ISBN-13: 978-0-9883878-5-0

This book contains statistics and information from the 2016 Survey of State Regulations for Home Inspectors. This survey was independently conducted, and the results are reprinted with permission. Figure 1, illustration of a drip leg, is reprinted with permission from InterNACHI; and figure 2, diagram of service drop clearances, is reprinted with permission from Carson Dunlop.

Disclaimer
This book is for educational purposes only. While the author has taken reasonable precautions in writing this book and believes that the facts presented in this book are accurate at the time of printing, the author and publisher make no representation or warranties with respect to accurateness or completeness of the contents of this book and disclaim all liability resulting from the use or application of any and all information, ideas, or advice in this book. The advice and counsel contained herein may not be suitable for every situation, and this book is not a substitute for hiring a professional home inspector. The author and the publisher disclaim liability for any loss of profit or any incidental, consequential, special, or other damages.

Expert Press

Expert Press
Little Rock, Arkansas
www.ExpertPress.net

www.ingramcontent.com/pod-product-compliance
Lightning Source LLC
Chambersburg PA
CBHW052211270326
41931CB00011B/2306
9780988387850